the **complete** *series*

5 Ingredients

WILEY

John Wiley & Sons, Inc.

Library of Congress Cataloging-in-Publication Data is available upon request.

ISBN 978-1-118-11977-8

Printed in China

10 9 8 7 6 5 4 3 2 1

Contents

Introduction

With our busy modern lifestyle, we often have little time for the preparation and cooking of the family meal. To deal with this problem, this cookbook has been produced using the minimum of ingredients and with recipes designed to be tasty, easy to prepare and quick to cook.

In order to make these recipes as tasty as possible using only 5 ingredients, our chefs have used some commercially available sauces and spices, all obtained to make the best possible meal with the minimum of fuss.

Long before modern cooking, our ancestors trapped and killed game and most probably ate it raw as they stripped the meat off the carcasses.

Somewhere in the distant past fire was introduced, and our ancestors became adept at cooking their kill on a stick over an open fire.

Some adventurous forerunners of the modern cook then found that by the addition of some plants, leaves and roots they could enhance the flavor of their meal.

As civilization progressed so did our cooking skills, so today we find that some gourmet recipes can have as many as 40 ingredients, and can take days to prepare and cook – totally impractical for most people.

While often looking to reduce our household costs, we certainly don't want to reduce the nutrition and taste of the meals we put on the table.

Our chefs and home economists have accepted the challenge to make tasty, nutritious, easy-to-prepare meals using the minimum of ingredients, and have produced this book full of great recipes using only 5 ingredients. We have not included salt and pepper in our ingredient lists, as we find that these two ingredients are used by everyone in a different manner – from none at all to excessive amounts.

You should also have a reasonably well-stocked pantry of herbs and spices, plus a selection of sauces – again, these can be used to suit the individual palate. Look through the displays in your local supermarket and choose a range that will suit your tastes.

While putting together a 5 ingredient cookbook is essentially not very difficult, making a 5 ingredient recipe that will satisfy all members of the family most definitely is.

We are assisted by the huge number of processed foods available at your supermarket, including sauces, jams, chutneys, mustards and canned or frozen fish, meat and vegetables.

We have broken the recipes up into chapters to make it easy to select the recipe you need for a particular occasion. We cover great breakfasts, entertaining dips and sauces, meat to feed the troops, seafood for any occasion, poultry for those who prefer white meat, pasta and rice, vegetarian dishes and some terrific desserts.

Breakfast and Brunch

When thinking breakfast the first thing that comes to mind – after coffee or tea, of course – is eggs. With an egg we can start the day right with a multitude of cooking ideas. We can scramble them, bake them, boil them, fry them or poach them. The old cry 'if there is and egg in the house there is a meal in the house' is just as true today as it was when first spoken over 100 years ago. However we have not just stopped at eggs! We have provided a number of tasty dishes in this chapter, all easy to prepare and quickly cooked – so let's get started!

Stuffed Portabella Mushrooms

200g/7 oz baby spinach leaves
4 large portabella mushrooms, gills removed
100g/3 oz feta cheese, crumbled
¼ cup sun-dried tomato pesto
freshly ground black pepper

1 Preheat the broiler.

2 Wash the spinach and cook in a medium saucepan over low heat until wilted.

3 Place the mushrooms on a baking sheet stem-side down and broil for 3 minutes.

4 Turn the mushrooms over and top with wilted spinach. Sprinkle with feta, pesto and freshly ground black pepper. Broil for an additional 3 minutes, until mushrooms are cooked and cheese is golden.

Serves 2 • Preparation 6 minutes • Cooking 6 minutes

French Toast with Strawberries

3 large eggs
4 slices sourdough bread, about an inch thick each
2 tablespoons milk
1½ cups strawberries, hulled and quartered
1 tablespoon powdered sugar

1 Preheat a large non-stick frying pan on medium-high heat.

2 Beat the eggs and milk in a medium bowl until combined.

3 Dip the bread into the egg mixture, then cook for 3 minutes on each side until golden.

4 Place the French toast onto two serving plates. Top with strawberries and dust with powdered sugar.

Serves 2 • Preparation 5 minutes • Cooking 6 minutes

Ham and Cheese Croissant

2 croissants, cut in half, horizontally
1 teaspoon Dijon mustard
2 slices honey-cured ham
4 slices fontina cheese
3 tablespoons tomato chutney

1 Preheat the broiler.
2 Toast the croissants, cut side up until lightly golden. Spread one side with mustard, layer with ham and cheese.
3 Toast again until melted. Top with chutney.

Serves 2 • Preparation 5 minutes • Cooking 8 minutes

Smoked Salmon Bagel

2 bagels, cut in half, horizontally
4 tablespoons crème fraîche or cream cheese
2 slices smoked salmon
arugula leaves
chopped chives

1 Toast bagels until lightly golden.
2 Spread with crème fraiche or cream cheese. Layer with smoked salmon, arugula, and chives.

Serves 2 • Preparation 5 minutes • Cooking 5 minutes

Poached Eggs with Creamed Spinach

200g/7 oz spinach, washed and chopped
½ cup heavy cream
pinch nutmeg
2 large eggs
2 slices multigrain bread, about an inch thick

1 Place the cream, nutmeg and spinach in a large saucepan on medium heat. Cook for 5–10 minutes until the cream has thickened to a saucy consistency.
2 Meanwhile, bring a medium saucepan of water to a simmer. Using a spoon, create a whirlpool and crack the eggs one at a time into the center. Poach for about 3 minutes, or until whites are slightly firm.
3 Toast bread slices until golden. Top with poached eggs and serve with spinach on the side.

Serves 2 • Preparation 10 minutes • Cooking 12 minutes

Basil and Feta Omelet

4 large eggs, separated
½ cup fresh basil leaves, torn
90g/3–4 oz feta cheese, crumbled
½ red onion, sliced
2 tablespoons olive oil

1 Preheat the broiler.
2 Beat the egg yolks in a medium bowl. In a separate bowl, whisk the whites until soft peaks form. Gently fold the whites into the yolks until combined.
3 Pour egg mixture into large ovenproof skillet. Cook for 2 minutes.
4 Broil for an additional 2 minutes until eggs are set and slightly golden. Slide out of the pan and top with feta, basil, and red onion.

Serves 2 • Preparation 5 minutes • Cooking 5 minutes
.

Rösti with Smoked Trout

400g/14 oz russet or Idaho potatoes, washed
45g/3 tablespoons butter, melted
freshly ground black pepper
50g/2 oz watercress
½ smoked trout, bones and skin removed

1 Place the unpeeled potatoes in a medium saucepan. Cover with cold water and bring
   to a boil. Cook for 10 minutes, drain and allow to cool completely. Peel and grate
   the potatoes and place in a medium bowl. Add freshly ground black pepper and the
   melted butter and toss to combine.

2 Preheat a large non-stick frying pan over medium-high heat. Place two mounds of
   potato onto the pan and flatten with a spatula. Cook for 10 minutes on both sides
   or until golden brown and crisp. Place röstis onto two serving plates. Top with
   watercress and smoked trout.

Serves 2 • Preparation 10 minutes • Cooking 20 minutes

Cannellini Beans and Tomatoes

800g/28 oz canned chopped tomatoes
400g/14 oz canned cannellini beans, drained
1 small red onion, chopped
¼ cup fresh Italian parsley, chopped
1 tablespoon chopped basil

1 Place the tomatoes, beans and onion in a small saucepan over medium-low heat.
   Cover and cook for 15–20 minutes. Remove the lid and cook for an additional
   5 minutes until the sauce has thickened slightly. Stir through parsley and basil
   and serve.

Serves 2 • Preparation 5 minutes • Cooking 25 minutes

Roasted Peaches with Yogurt and Almonds

2 ripe peaches, halved and stones removed
2 tablespoons flaked almonds, toasted
1½ tablespoons shaved coconut, lightly toasted
½ cup yogurt
1 teaspoon sugar

1 Preheat the oven to 350°F/180°C.

2 Place the peach halves on a baking sheet cut-side down and bake for 10 minutes or until softened slightly. Turn the peaches over and bake for an additional 5 minutes.

3 Combine the almonds and coconut in a small bowl. Arrange the peach halves cut-side up on two serving plates or bowls. Mix yogurt and sugar together. Top with a dollop of yogurt and sprinkle with almonds and coconut.

Serves 2 • Preparation 5 minutes • Cooking 15 minutes

Potato Cakes with Strawberry Jam

350g/¾ lb potatoes, peeled and quartered
45g/3 tablespoons butter
1 tablespoon cream
¾ cup all-purpose flour
4 tablespoons strawberry jam

1 Place the potatoes in a medium saucepan. Cover with cold water and bring to a boil. Cook for 8–10 minutes or until tender. Drain well and return to the saucepan. Add one-third of the butter and cream and mash. Let cool slightly.

2 Turn the mashed potatoes out onto a clean, floured work surface. Gradually add the flour, kneading until a smooth dough is formed. Roll out to ½ in/1cm thickness and cut into triangles.

3 Preheat a large frying pan on medium heat. Melt the remaining butter in the pan and cook the potato cakes for 3 minutes on each side or until browned. Serve hot with strawberry jam.

Serves 2 • Preparation 10 minutes • Cooking 16 minutes

Yogurt Parfait

100g/3½ oz pecans
2 cups vanilla yogurt
1 teaspoon honey
1 teaspoon ground cinnamon
3 cups blueberries

1 Preheat the oven to 350°F/180°C.
2 Spread the pecans on a baking sheet and toast in the oven for 10 minutes or until lightly toasted. Coarsely chop.
3 Combine the yogurt, honey and cinnamon in a small bowl. Layer the yogurt, blueberries and pecans in two glass serving bowls or cups.

Serves 2 • Preparation 5 minutes • Cooking 10 minutes

Sweet Baked Ricotta

300g/10 oz ricotta cheese
1 large egg, lightly beaten
¼ cup flaked almonds, lightly toasted
½ teaspoon finely grated orange zest
4 tablespoons mixed berry jam

1 Preheat the oven to 325°F/170°C.
2 Mix the ricotta, egg, almonds, orange zest and jam together in a medium bowl.
3 Spoon the mixture into two 1-cup capacity ovenproof ramekins. Place ramekins onto a baking sheet and bake for 40 minutes or until set. Remove from the oven and let cool. Serve at room temperature.

Serves 2 • Preparation 5 minutes • Cooking 40 minutes

Dips and Sauces

At your next dinner party, why not make up a tasty dip to start the occasion, or maybe just a few drinks with a dip to tease the palate? And how about using one of these great sauce recipes? There's a mint sauce to go with your lamb, mayonnaise to go with chicken, cocktail sauce to suit those crispy fresh prawns, or a salsa for that great barbecued steak. The ideas here are simple, easy to prepare and most of all are very tasty indeed.

Eggplant Dip

2 medium eggplant
4 tablespoons extra virgin olive oil
1 clove garlic, finely chopped
2 tablespoons lemon juice
1 French baguette, cut into ½ in/1cm slices

1 Preheat the broiler.
2 Prick the eggplants with a knife to prevent them from bursting. Place under the broiler and cook for 5 minutes, turning occasionally, until soft. Peel the eggplant and place the flesh in a colander. Mash to a purée using a fork or the back of a spoon, allowing the juices to drain out.
3 Transfer the eggplant purée to a medium bowl. Add the olive oil, garlic and lemon juice, stirring to combine. Serve in a small bowl accompanied with chunks of bread.

Serves 4 • Preparation 5 minutes • Cooking 5 minutes

Spiced Yogurt Dip

½ teaspoon cumin seeds
¼ teaspoon ground turmeric
pinch allspice
300g/10 oz plain yogurt
1 tablespoon lemon juice

1 Cook the spices in a small frying pan over medium heat until fragrant. Remove from the heat and let cool.
2 Place the yogurt in a small bowl. Add the spices and lemon juice and stir to combine. Transfer to a small serving dish.

Serves 4 • Preparation 5 minutes • Cooking 5 minutes

Skordalia

Skordalia

500g/18 oz potatoes
8 cloves garlic, crushed
½ cup extra virgin olive oil
2 tablespoons lemon juice
½ teaspoon lemon pepper

1 Peel and cut the potatoes into cubes. Place in a medium saucepan, cover with water and bring to a boil. Cook for 10–15 minutes until tender. Drain and leave to cool a little.
2 Place the potato, garlic, olive oil, lemon juice and pepper in a food processor. Blend until smooth and creamy. Add a little of the cooking water if it's too thick.

Serves 4 • Preparation 10 minutes • Cooking 15 minutes

Smoked Salmon Dip

80g/3 oz smoked salmon
1 teaspoon lemon juice
1 tablespoon capers
200g/7 oz cream cheese, softened
¼ cup sour cream

1 Place the smoked salmon, lemon juice and capers in a food processor and pulse until finely chopped. Add the cream cheese and sour cream and process until smooth.

Serves 4 • Preparation 5 minutes

White Bean Dip

400g/14 oz canned cannellini beans, drained
2 tablespoons lemon juice
2 tablespoons extra virgin olive oil
½ teaspoon ground cumin
½ teaspoon ground black pepper

1 Place the cannellini beans, lemon juice, olive oil, cumin and black pepper in a food processor. Process until smooth, adding a little water if it's too thick. Transfer to a small serving dish.

Serves 4 • Preparation 10

Taramasalata

200g/7 oz fresh smoked cod roe
½ teaspoon black pepper
1 slice white bread, crust removed
1 tablespoon lemon juice
1 cup light olive oil

1 Place the roe in a small bowl, cover with cold water and soak for 2 hours. Drain, peel off the skin and place the roe in a food processor with the black pepper
2 Moisten the bread with cold water and squeeze out any excess. Add the bread and lemon juice to the roe and pulse until puréed. With processor on medium-high speed, gradually pour in the oil. Go slowly otherwise it will curdle. Scrape down the sides and process until combined and thick. Transfer to a small serving dish.

Serves 4 • Preparation 2 hours 10 minutes

White Bean Dip

Mexican Salsa

Mexican Salsa

1 green bell pepper, halved lengthwise and seeded
2 large red chilies, halved lengthwise and seeded
1 clove garlic, crushed
2 large ripe tomatoes, diced
3 tablespoons extra virgin olive oil

1 Chop the bell pepper and finely chop the chili. Combine the bell pepper, chili, garlic, tomato and olive oil in a medium bowl. Stir to combine. Transfer to a small serving bowl.

Serves 4 • Preparation 5 minutes

Tapenade

150g/5 oz pitted black olives
100g/3½ oz pitted kalamata olives
1 clove garlic, crushed
2 tablespoons capers
1 tablespoon lemon juice

1 Place the olives, garlic, capers and lemon juice in a food processor. Blend until smooth. Transfer to a small serving bowl.

Serves 4 • Preparation 5 minutes

Blue Cheese Walnut Dip

150g/5 oz soft blue cheese
200g/7 oz crème fraîche or sour cream
75g/2–3 oz walnuts, lightly toasted and coarsely chopped
¼ cup fresh basil leaves, finely chopped
crisp crunchy bread to dip

1 Place the blue cheese and half the crème fraîche in a small bowl. Stir until combined. Add the remaining crème fraîche, walnuts and basil and mix well. Garnish with a few extra walnuts. Serve with crunchy bread to dip.

Serves 4 • Preparation 5 minutes

Spicy Red Pepper Dip

4 red bell peppers
1 garlic clove, crushed
¼ cup extra virgin olive oil
1 tablespoon lemon juice
2 teaspoons sambal oelek or chili paste

1 Preheat broiler. Broil the bell peppers until the skins have blackened all over. Place in a bowl and cover with plastic wrap for 10 minutes. Remove the skins and seeds and coarsely chop.
2 Place the bell pepper, garlic, olive oil, lemon juice and sambal oelek in a food processor. Blend until smooth, then transfer to a small serving dish.

Serves 4 • Preparation 20 minutes • Cooking 10 minutes

Artichoke Dip

1 large red onion
400g/14 oz marinated artichokes, drained and liquid reserved
4 capers
200g/7 oz cream cheese
4 sprigs fresh oregano, leaves removed and finely chopped

1 Preheat the oven to 350°F/190°C.
2 Place the onion on a small baking sheet and roast for 35–40 minutes until softened. Leave to cool a little, then peel and coarsely chop.
3 Place the onion, artichokes, capers and cream cheese in a food processor. Blend until smooth, adding a little of the reserved liquid if it's too thick. Stir through the oregano and transfer to a small serving dish.

Serves 4 • Preparation 10 minutes • Cooking 40 minutes

Raita Dip

300g/10 oz plain yogurt
¼ cup fresh cilantro leaves, finely chopped
¼ cup fresh mint leaves, finely chopped
½ tablespoon lime juice
½ tablespoon lemon juice

1 Place the yogurt in a small bowl, then add the cilantro and mint. Add the lime and lemon juice and stir to combine. Transfer to a small serving dish.

Serves 4 • Preparation 5 minutes

Tartar Sauce

1 cup mayonnaise
1 large dill pickle, finely chopped
1 tablespoon capers, finely chopped
1 tablespoon lemon juice
¼ teaspoon ground white pepper

1 Place the mayonnaise in a small bowl, then add the pickle and capers. Pour in the lemon juice and white pepper and stir to combine. Transfer to a small serving dish.

Serves 4 • Preparation 5 minutes

Garlic Aïoli

1 large bulb garlic
1 cup mayonnaise
1 tablespoon lemon juice
¼ cup fresh parsley leaves, finely chopped
¼ teaspoon lemon pepper

1 Preheat the oven to 375°F/190°C.
2 Place the garlic bulb on a small roasting tray and roast for 30 minutes or until soft. Leave to cool. Squeeze the garlic out of its skin into a small bowl, then mash with the back of a fork.
3 Add the mayonnaise, lemon juice, lemon pepper and parsley and stir to combine.

Serves 4 • Preparation 5 minutes • Cooking 30 minutes

Tartar Sauce

Lentil Dip

Lentil Dip

250g/9 oz yellow or red lentils
1½ teaspoons cumin seeds
1 clove garlic, minced
3 tablespoons extra virgin olive oil
½ tablespoon lemon juice

1 Place the lentils in a medium saucepan and cover with double their volume of water. Bring to a boil and cook for 15 minutes. Add more water if necessary and continue cooking until they form a soft purée. Let cool.

2 Cook the cumin seeds in a small frying pan over medium heat until fragrant. Add 1 teaspoon of the cumin seeds, the garlic, lemon juice and olive oil to the lentil purée. Stir to combine. Transfer to a small serving bowl and garnish with the remaining cumin seeds.

Serves 4 • Preparation 10 minutes • Cooking 25 minutes

Homemade Mayonnaise

3 large egg yolks, at room temperature
1 teaspoon Dijon mustard
2 tablespoons lemon juice

¼ teaspoon white pepper
¾ cup canola oil

1 Place the egg yolks, mustard, pepper and lemon juice in a food processor and pulse to combine. With the motor running, add the oil in a thin stream until incorporated. Add a little hot water if mayonnaise is too thick. Transfer to a serving dish or storage jar and refrigerate.

Mayonnaise will keep for about 1 week in the refrigerator.

Serves 4 • Preparation 10 minutes

Seafood

One of the easiest and quickest ingredients to cook is seafood, especially fish. This wonderful resource is both nutritiously good for you and tasty as well. There are many types of seafood suitable for frying, poaching, grilling, baking and even eating raw. You can also buy filets, cutlets, steaks and whole fish to suit your taste. You do not have to buy the most expensive fish to get a terrific meal – in fact, we have purposely selected the recipes in this chapter to cover a variety of budgets.

Scallops with Capers and Lemons

32 scallops, in half shells
3 tablespoons capers, finely chopped
juice and zest of 2 lemons
60g/2 oz butter, cubed
freshly ground black pepper

1 Preheat the broiler.
2 Loosen the scallops from their shells by sliding a small knife between the shell and the scallop. Arrange the scallops on 2 baking sheets.
3 Combine the capers, lemon zest and juice in a small bowl. Spoon the caper mixture over the scallops and top with a small cube of butter.
4 Broil the scallops for 4 minutes, or until cooked through. Arrange on four serving plates and sprinkle with black pepper.

Serves 4 • Preparation 10 minutes • Cooking 4 minutes

Cod with Mango Salsa

2 mangos, peeled
2 limes
1 lemon
¾ cup fresh cilantro leaves
4 cod filets, about 200g/7 oz each

1 Dice the mango and place in a medium bowl. Add cilantro and the zest and juice from one lemon and one lime. Stir to combine. Cut the remaining lime into quarters.

2 Preheat a large non-stick frying pan on medium-high heat. Cook the fish for 2 minutes on each side or until flesh flakes easily. Serve immediately with mango and lime wedges.

Serves 4 • Preparation 10 minutes • Cooking 4 minutes

Baked Whole Trout

1kg/2 lb baby red or Yukon gold potatoes
¼ cup olive oil
4 small whole trout, scaled and cleaned
2 bunches thyme, washed and ends trimmed
juice of one lemon

1 Preheat the oven to 375°F/190°C.

2 Place the potatoes in a medium saucepan. Cover with cold water and bring to a boil. Cook for 5 minutes, then drain and place on a large baking sheet. Toss with 4 tablespoons of olive oil and roast for 20–25 minutes, turning once until golden brown.

3 Tear off four pieces of aluminium foil large enough to wrap each trout. Score the trout 3 times on each side. Coat in the remaining oil and place onto the foil. Pour lemon juice over it. Sprinkle a few thyme leaves over the fish and stuff the remaining thyme inside the cavity. Enclose the trout in the foil and place onto baking sheets. Bake for 15–20 minutes until flesh flakes easily. Serve with the potatoes.

Serves 4 • Preparation 20 minutes • Cooking 50 minutes

Steamed Ginger Fish

1½ cups basmati rice
2 in/5cm piece ginger, peeled and sliced
12 kaffir lime leaves, finely sliced
¼ teaspoon ground coriander
4 firm white fish filets, about 200g/7 oz each

1 Combine the rice with 2¼ cups water in a saucepan. Bring to a boil, reduce heat to low, cover and cook for 15 minutes. Remove pan from heat, allow to stand covered for 10 minutes.
2 Meanwhile, line a large steamer with parchment. Make holes in the paper so that the steam can penetrate. Fill the base of the steamer with 2 in/4cm of water, place over high heat, bring to a boil, then reduce to a simmer.
3 Sprinkle half the ginger, the coriander and lime leaves on the prepared paper and place the fish on top. Top with the remaining ginger and lime, cover and cook for 6–10 minutes until the flesh flakes easily. Serve the fish immediately with rice.

Serves 4 • Preparation 25 minutes • Cooking 25 minutes

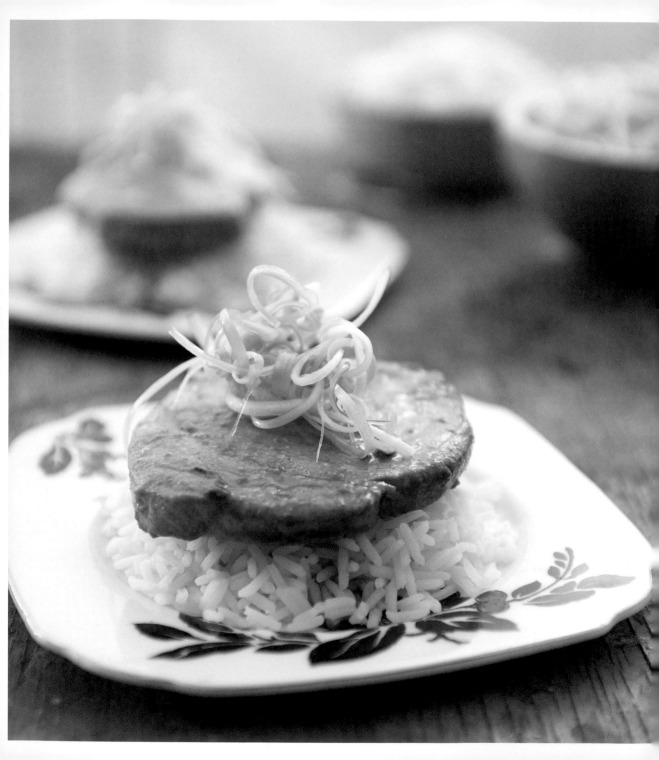

Teriyaki Fish

4 swordfish steaks, about 150g/5 oz each
1 cup teriyaki sauce
1 tablespoon freshly grated ginger
1½ cups basmati rice
4 green onions, trimmed

1   Place the fish in a medium bowl and coat in teriyaki sauce and ginger. Cover and refrigerate for 1 hour.

2   Combine the rice with 2¼ cups water in a saucepan. Bring to a boil, reduce heat to low, cover and cook for 15 minutes. Remove pan from heat, allow to stand covered for 10 minutes.

3   Cut the green onions into 2½ in/6cm pieces. Thinly slice each piece lengthwise into strips.

4   Preheat a large non-stick frying pan over medium-high heat. Take the fish out of the marinade, reserving the marinade, and cook for 2 minutes on each side or until browned. Add the reserved marinade and gently simmer, basting until the fish is covered in a glossy glaze.

5   Divide the rice and fish evenly among four serving plates and top with green onions.

Serves 4 • Preparation 1 hour 25 minutes • Cooking 25 minutes

Red Curry Fish

1½ tablespoons red curry paste
1 cup coconut milk
½ teaspoon ground coriander
8 baby bok choy, halved lengthwise
4 firm white fish filets, about 200g/7 oz each

1 Preheat a large non-stick frying pan over medium heat. Add the curry paste and cook until aromatic. Pour in the coconut milk and coriander, reduce the heat and gently simmer for 2 minutes until thickened slightly.

2 Meanwhile, fill the base of a steamer with 2 in/4cm of water and place over high heat, bring to a boil and then reduce to a simmer. Place the bok choy on the steamer tray, cover and cook for 3 minutes or until tender. Add the filets to the curry sauce and cook, basting with sauce for 3–4 minutes until cooked through.

3 Carefully lift the fish out of the sauce and place on serving plates with the bok choy. Pour over the sauce and serve.

Serves 4 • Preparation 15 minutes • Cooking 10 minutes

Cajun Snapper

80g/3 oz butter, melted
2 tablespoons Cajun seasoning
4 snapper filets, about 200g/7 oz each
1 cup plain yogurt
1 teaspoon lemon juice

1 Preheat a large non-stick frying pan on medium-high heat. Combine the butter and Cajun seasoning in a small bowl. Coat the fish in the spice and cook for 2 minutes on each side or until flesh flakes easily.

2 Mix the lemon juice with the yogurt until combined.

3 Serve immediately with yogurt on the side.

Serves 4 • Preparation 5 minutes • Cooking 4 minutes

Spicy Shrimp and Noodles

24 raw shrimp, peeled with tails intact
3 tablespoons sambal oelek (chili garlic sauce)
400g/14 oz vermicelli rice noodles
2 tablespoons vegetable oil
2 red bell peppers, seeded and thinly sliced

1 In a medium bowl, combine shrimp and sambal oelek. Toss to coat. Cover and refrigerate for 1–2 hours.

2 Place the noodles in a medium bowl, cover with boiling water and soak for 5–10 minutes until softened. Drain and set aside.

3 Heat the oil in a large non-stick frying pan over high heat. Cook the shrimp for 1½ minutes on each side or until they turn pink and begin to firm up. Add the bell pepper and the noodles and toss to combine. Serve immediately.

Serves 4 • Preparation 2 hours 25 minutes • Cooking 15 minutes

Poultry

How many ways can we cook a chicken? There must be millions of recipes in the world that cook poultry in different ways, or so it seems. Just by the addition of a different herb, sauce or cooking method we can change the flavor of this wonderful food. In this chapter we have produced very simply prepared dishes with the minimum of fuss and ingredients, yet these recipes are as tasty as those with a multitude of ingredients. We are sure that you will enjoy our selection.

Chicken, Fennel and Orange Salad

4 boneless, skinless chicken breasts
1 tablespoon vegetable oil
3 oranges
1 fennel bulb, core removed and thinly sliced
150g/5 oz watercress

1 Heat the oil in a large non-stick frying pan on medium-high heat.
2 Cook the chicken breasts for 5–7 minutes on each side until cooked through. Remove from the heat and leave to rest for 5 minutes.
3 Peel and segment the orange over a bowl, collecting the juice that drips as you work.
4 Slice the chicken and place in a large bowl. Add the orange segments, fennel and watercress. Pour in enough of the reserved orange juice to moisten as a dressing. Toss to combine and serve.

Serves 4 • Preparation 20 minutes • Cooking 20 minutes

Pancetta-Wrapped Chicken

4 tablespoons basil pesto
4 large basil leaves
4 chicken breast filets
8 slices pancetta
12 cherry tomatoes on the vine

1 Preheat the oven to 375°F/190°C.
2 Spread the pesto over the chicken breasts. Place a basil leaf on each breast. Lay two slices of pancetta over each breast and wrap around.
3 Preheat a large non-stick frying pan on medium-high heat. Cook the chicken breasts for 2 minutes on each side or until golden brown. Transfer to a baking sheet and bake for an additional 15–20 minutes or until cooked through.
4 Place the tomatoes on a baking sheet and bake for 10–15 minutes until they begin to soften. Serve with the chicken.

Serves 4 • Preparation 20 minutes • Cooking 40 minutes

Roast Lemon Chicken with Couscous

1 whole roaster chicken (2kg/4–5 lb)
3 lemons
2 sprigs thyme
1¾ cups chicken stock
1½ cups couscous

1 Preheat the oven 375°F/190°C.
2 Wash chicken and pat dry. Tie the chicken legs together using kitchen string and place in a large roasting pan.
3 Juice two of the lemons into a small bowl and add ¼ cup of the chicken stock. Pour over the chicken. Cut the remaining lemon in half and place one half in the chicken cavity with the thyme. Slice the remaining half and arrange over the chicken. Roast, basting occasionally, for 1½ hours or until juices run clear from the thigh when pricked with a skewer. Let rest for 10 minutes before carving.
4 Pour the chicken stock into a small saucepan and bring to a boil. Add the couscous, remove from the heat and cover with plastic wrap. Let it stand for 5 minutes or until liquid is completely absorbed. Stir gently with a fork to separate the grains.

Serves 4 • Preparation 20 minutes • Cooking 1 hour 35 minutes

Garlic Chicken

90g/6½ tablespoons butter, softened
6 cloves garlic, crushed
½ cup fresh parsley leaves, finely chopped
4 chicken breasts on the bone, skin on
1 tablespoon oregano leaves

1 Preheat the oven to 350°F/180°C.
2 Place the butter, garlic, oregano and parsley in a small bowl and stir to combine.
3 Put the garlic butter under the chicken skin. Place the chicken breasts skin-side up and bake for 20–25 minutes until cooked through.

Serves 4 • Preparation 10 minutes • Cooking 25 minutes

Sweet Orange Chicken

4 boneless, skinless chicken breasts
6 tablespoons orange marmalade
1 teaspoon lemon zest
150g/5 oz arugula leaves
80g/3 oz feta cheese, cubed

1 Preheat the oven to 350°F/180°C.
2 Place the chicken breasts in a large baking sheet lined with parchment paper. Coat each breast in the orange marmalade and lemon zest. Cover with foil and bake for 10 minutes. Remove the foil and bake for an additional 10–15 minutes or until cooked through.
3 Serve the chicken with the arugula and feta.

Serves 4 • Preparation 10 minutes • Cooking 25 minutes

Chicken Yakitori

1kg/2 lb boneless, skinless chicken thighs, cut into 1½ in/3cm pieces
¾ cup teriyaki sauce
1½ cups basmati rice
3 tablespoons sesame seeds, toasted
1 teaspoon sesame oil

1 Place the chicken pieces in a medium bowl. Add the teriyaki sauce and toss to coat. Cover and refrigerate for 1–2 hours or until required.
2 Carefully thread the chicken onto skewers.
3 Preheat a grill pan to medium-high heat.
4 Combine the rice with 2¼ cups water in a saucepan. Bring to a boil, reduce heat to low, cover and cook for 15 minutes. Remove pan from heat, allow to stand covered for 10 minutes. Stir in the toasted sesame seeds.
5 Brush the chicken with sesame oil and cook for 5 minutes on each side or until cooked through. Serve with the rice.

Serves 4 • Preparation 2 hours 25 minutes • Cooking 20 minutes

Asian Chicken Noodle Salad

2 boneless, skinless chicken breasts
1 tablespoon vegetable oil
400g/14 oz vermicelli rice noodles
250g/9 oz snowpeas
½ cup sweet chili sauce

1 Heat the oil in a large non-stick frying pan on medium-high heat.
2 Cook the chicken breasts for 5–7 minutes on each side until cooked through. Remove from the heat and let rest for 5 minutes.
3 Place the noodles in a medium bowl, cover with boiling water and soak until softened. Drain and set aside.
4 Blanch the snowpeas in boiling water for 30 seconds. Plunge into ice water to stop the cooking process. Slice thinly lengthwise.
5 Shred the chicken and place in a large bowl. Add the noodles, snowpeas and chili sauce. Toss to combine and serve.

Serves 4 • Preparation 20 minutes • Cooking 22 minutes

Chicken Lo Mein

400g/14 oz hokkien noodles
1 bunch gai lan (Chinese broccoli), cut into short lengths
3 chicken thigh filets, sliced
¾ cup oyster sauce
1 clove garlic, crushed

1 Cook the noodles in a large pot of boiling water according to packet instructions. Drain and set aside.
2 Place a medium saucepan of water on high heat and bring to a boil. Blanch the gai lan for 1 minute and drain.
3 Preheat a large non-stick frying pan or wok on high heat.
4 Add the chicken and cook for 2 minutes or until browned. Add the noodles, gai lan, garlic and oyster sauce and toss to combine. Cook for an additional 5 minutes or until chicken is cooked and sauce is heated through.

Serves 4 • Preparation 15 minutes • Cooking 10 minutes

Honey Mustard Chicken with Roast Potatoes

4 chicken leg quarters
¾ cup honey mustard marinade*
500g/1 lb baby red or Yukon gold potatoes
3 tablespoons olive oil
1 tablespoon lemon juice

1 Place the chicken in a medium bowl and coat with marinade. Cover with plastic wrap and refrigerate for 2 hours or until required.

2 Preheat the oven to 400°F/200°C.

3 Place the potatoes in a large saucepan and cover with water. Bring to a boil and cook for 5 minutes. Drain and place in a roasting dish. Pour in the olive oil and lemon juice and toss to coat. Roast for 30 minutes or until golden brown.

4 Preheat a large non-stick frying pan on medium-high heat. Cook the chicken legs for 2 minutes on each side or until browned. Transfer to an ovenproof dish and bake for 20 minutes or until cooked through. Serve with the roast potatoes.

*You can use a pre-made marinade or make your own by combining 2 parts Dijon mustard, 2 parts honey, and 1 part soy sauce.

Serves 4 • Preparation 2 hours 20 minutes • Cooking 1 hour

Duck with Plum Sauce

4 duck breasts
½ cup Asian plum sauce
1 teaspoon kecap manis*
1½ cups basmati rice
4 bok choy, trimmed and leaves separated

1 Use a sharp knife to score the skin of the duck breasts at ½ in/1cm intervals. Place the duck in a medium bowl with kecap manis and plum sauces and coat duck. Cover with plastic wrap and refrigerate for 1–2 hours or until required.

2 Combine the rice with 2¼ cups water in a saucepan. Bring to a boil, reduce heat to low, cover and cook for 15 minutes. Remove pan from heat, allow to stand covered for 10 minutes.

3 Preheat the oven to 350°F/180°C. Preheat a large non-stick frying pan over medium-high heat. Cook the duck, skin-side down, for 3 minutes or until golden brown. Turn over and cook for an additional minute. Transfer to an ovenproof dish and bake for 8 minutes for medium, or until cooked to your liking. Cover with foil and rest for 5 minutes.

4 Place a medium saucepan of water on high heat and bring to a boil. Blanch the bok choy for 1 minute, then drain.

*Kecap manis is a sweet soy sauce that you can find at Asian markets. If you can't find it, you can substitute one part molasses and two parts soy sauce.

Serves 4 • Preparation 2 hours 20 minutes • Cooking 30 minutes

Five-Spice Duck

4 duck breasts
2 tablespoons Chinese five-spice powder
1 tablespoon sesame oil
1 teaspoon ground ginger
1 Napa cabbage, chopped

1 Preheat the oven to 350°F/180°C.
2 Use a sharp knife to score the skin of the duck breasts at ½ in/1cm intervals. Rub the duck with five-spice powder and set aside for 15 minutes to develop the flavors.
3 Preheat a large non-stick frying pan over medium-high heat. Cook the duck, skin-side down, for 3 minutes or until golden brown. Turn over and cook for an additional minute. Transfer to an ovenproof dish and bake for 8 minutes for medium, or until cooked to your liking. Cover with foil and rest for 5 minutes.
4 Preheat a wok or non-stick frying pan on medium-high heat. Add the sesame oil and ginger and stir-fry the cabbage until tender. Serve the duck with the cabbage.

Serves 4 • Preparation 25 minutes • Cooking 20 minutes

Meat

Just look in your butcher's window or your supermarket's display cabinets and you will be amazed at the huge variety and different cuts of meat available. With so many cuts and varieties to choose from, you can easily be confused as to the selection required to make an interesting, tasty meal. Look through these recipes, make your selection, then visit the market to buy the correct cut and variety to suit the meal you wish to prepare. This will not only save time but will also save money as these recipes are designed to stretch the family budget.

Yogurt-Marinated Lamb Kebabs

700g/1½ lb lamb loin, cut into cubes
1 cup plain yogurt
1 teaspoon lemon juice
1½ cups chicken stock
1½ cups couscous

1 Place the lamb, lemon juice and yogurt in a medium bowl and stir to coat. Cover with plastic wrap and refrigerate for 2 hours or until required.

2 Soak 8 bamboo skewers in water to prevent them from burning. Preheat the barbecue to medium heat.

3 Thread the lamb onto the skewers. Cook, turning occasionally, for 6–8 minutes or until cooked to your liking.

4 Pour the chicken stock into a small saucepan and bring to a boil. Add the couscous, remove from the heat and cover with plastic wrap. Let it stand for 5 minutes or until liquid is completely absorbed. Stir gently with a fork to separate the grains. Serve the skewers with the couscous.

Serves 4 • Preparation 2 hours 15 minutes • Cooking 15 minutes

Pork with Prosciutto and Pears

4 bone-in pork chops
1 teaspoon ground cumin seeds
6 slices prosciutto, torn
6 ripe pears, cored and sliced
4 tablespoons apple cider

1 Preheat the oven to 400°F/200°C.

2 Preheat a large non-stick frying pan on medium-high heat.

3 Sprinkle pork with cumin seeds and cook the pork for 2 minutes on each side or until browned. Transfer to a baking sheet and cook for an additional 10–15 minutes or until cooked to your liking. Transfer to a plate, cover and rest for 5 minutes.

4 In the same pan, cook the prosciutto for 1–2 minutes or until crisp. Remove from the pan and set aside. Add the pears to the pan and cook, turning occasionally, for 3–4 minutes or until golden and tender. Remove from the pan and set aside with the prosciutto. Pour the apple cider into the pan and gently simmer, stirring to de-glaze the pan. Return the pears and prosciutto to the pan and toss to combine.

5 Serve the pork cutlets with the pear slices and prosciutto.

Serves 4 • Preparation 10 minutes • Cooking 30 minutes

Rack of Lamb with Smoky Eggplant

4 large eggplant
3 cloves garlic, crushed
300g/10 oz potatoes, peeled and coarsely chopped
4 racks of lamb, French trimmed, about 250g/9 oz each
¼ cup dukkah*

1 Preheat the broiler.
2 Preheat the oven to 375°F/190°C.
3 Prick the eggplant with a fork, and place on a baking sheet with the garlic. Broil, turning occasionally, for 15 minutes until skin has blackened and insides are tender. Remove and set aside to cool. Cut the eggplants in half lengthwise. Scoop the flesh out into a medium bowl and mash with a fork. Set aside and keep warm.
4 Place the potatoes in a medium saucepan. Cover with cold water and bring to a boil. Cook for 5–10 minutes or until tender. Drain, return to the saucepan and mash. Add the eggplant and stir to combine.
5 Coat the lamb in dukkah and roast for 25 minutes for medium or until cooked to your liking. Transfer to a plate, cover and rest for 5 minutes. Serve with mashed eggplant.

*Dukkah is an Egyptian dry spice mixture of chopped nuts and seeds. It's available at specialty food stores.

Serves 4 • Preparation 15 minutes • Cooking 50 minutes

Chinese Pork

⅓ cup hoisin sauce
4 tablespoons Chinese five-spice powder
1 kg/2½ lb pork tenderloin
2 bunches baby bok choy, cut in half lengthwise
¼ cup water

1 Combine the hoisin sauce and five-spice powder in a medium bowl. Add the pork, stir to coat, cover and refrigerate for 2 hours or until required.
2 Preheat grill to medium heat.
3 Cook the pork for 5–6 minutes on each side or until cooked to your liking. Transfer to a plate, cover and rest for 5 minutes.
4 Heat water in a wok over high heat. Cook the bok choy for 1–2 minutes or until tender.
5 Thickly slice the pork and serve with the bok choy.

Serves 4 • Preparation 2 hours 5 minutes • Cooking 15 minutes

Pork and Appleslaw

1 kg/2½ lb pork tenderloin
2 teaspoons sesame oil
3 Granny Smith apples, grated
¼ Savoy cabbage, thinly shredded
5 tablespoons honey mustard mayonnaise*

1 Preheat grill to medium heat.
2 Sprinkle pork with sesame oil and cook the pork for 5–6 minutes on each side or until cooked to your liking. Transfer to a plate, cover and rest for 5 minutes.
3 Place the apple and cabbage in a medium bowl. Add the honey mustard mayonnaise and stir to combine. Thickly slice the pork and serve with appleslaw.

*Honey mustard mayonnaise makes a great dipping sauce for chicken fingers. Make your own by combining ¾ cup mayonnaise, ¼ cup honey and 2 tablespoons of your favorite mustard. If you want to kick up the flavor, add a teaspoon of prepared horseradish, too.

Serves 4 • Preparation 15 minutes • Cooking 15 minutes

Prosciutto-Wrapped Steaks with Mashed Sweet Potatoes

1kg/2 lb sweet potato, peeled and coarsely chopped
1 teaspoon nutmeg
4 filet mignon steaks, about 180g/6 oz each
8 slices prosciutto
2 tablespoons whole grain mustard

1 Preheat the oven to 375°F/190°C.

2 Place the sweet potato in a medium saucepan, cover with cold water and bring to a boil. Cook for 10 minutes or until tender. Drain, return to the saucepan and mash with the nutmeg. Keep warm.

3 Preheat a large non-stick frying pan on high heat.

4 Cook the steaks for 1 minute on each side or until browned. Remove from the heat and allow to cool slightly.

5 Wrap two pieces of prosciutto around each beef filet, securing with a toothpick.

6 Place the beef on a baking sheet and bake for 8–10 minutes or until done to your liking. Transfer to a plate, cover and rest for 5 minutes.

7 Serve the steaks with sweet potatoes and whole grain mustard.

Serves 4 • Preparation 15 minutes • Cooking 20–25 minutes

Ginger Pork and Noodles

400g/14 oz udon noodles
1 tablespoon vegetable oil
600g/1½ lb pork tenderloin, thinly sliced
2 in/5cm piece fresh ginger, peeled and grated
⅓ cup oyster sauce

1 Place a medium saucepan of water on high heat and bring to a boil. Cook the
   noodles according to the packet directions and drain.

2 Heat the oil in a large non-stick frying pan on medium-high heat.

3 Cook the pork and ginger, stirring occasionally, for 2 minutes or until browned.
   Add the oyster sauce and cook for an additional 2 minutes. Add the noodles and
   toss to combine.

Serves 4 • Preparation 10 minutes • Cooking 15 minutes

Mustard Beef Tenderloin

1½ kg/3 lb beef tenderloin, trimmed off fat
¼ cup olive oil
1 clove garlic, crushed
½ cup whole grain mustard
1kg/2 lb baby red or Yukon gold potatoes

1 Preheat the oven to 400°F/200°C.
2 Preheat a large non-stick frying pan on high heat.
3 Brush the beef filet with olive oil and crushed garlic and cook, turning occasionally, for 5 minutes or until browned all over.
4 Transfer to a large roasting dish. Rub the mustard over the beef and bake for 40 minutes for medium-rare, or until cooked to your liking. Remove from the oven, cover and rest for 10 minutes.
5 Place the potatoes in a large saucepan, cover with cold water and bring to a boil. Cook for 10 minutes or until tender. Drain.
6 Heat the remaining oil in a large frying pan. Add the potatoes and cook for 3–4 minutes or until golden brown.

Serves 8 • Preparation 10 minutes • Cooking 1 hour 10 minutes

Steaks with Mushroom Cream Sauce

4 filet mignon steaks, about 180g/6 oz each
2 teaspoons vegetable oil
400g/14 oz mixed wild mushrooms
⅓ cup beef stock
⅓ cup heavy cream

1 Preheat the oven to 375°F/190°C.

2 Heat the oil in a large non-stick frying pan on medium-high heat.

3 Cook the steaks for 4–5 minutes on each side or until done to your liking. Transfer to a plate, cover and rest for 5 minutes.

4 In the same pan, cook the mushrooms, stirring, for 3 minutes or until golden brown. Add the beef stock and cream and bring to a boil. Decrease the heat and simmer for 2 minutes or until thickened slightly.

Serves 4 • Preparation 5 minutes • Cooking 20 minutes

Beef Stir-Fry

600g/1½ lb beef tenderloin, thinly sliced
1 tablespoon vegetable oil
1½ teaspoons Sichuan pepper
2 bunches gai lan (Chinese broccoli), cut into 2 in/5cm lengths
½ cup char siu sauce*

1 Heat the oil in a large non-stick frying pan on high heat.
2 Place the beef and Sichuan pepper in a medium bowl and stir to combine. Add the beef to the pan and cook, stirring occasionally, for 1–2 minutes or until browned. Add the gai lan and cook for an additional 2 minutes. Pour in the char siu sauce, heat through and toss to combine.
3 Divide the beef stir-fry evenly among four serving bowls.

*Char siu sauce is a specialty barbecue sauce made with soy sauce, honey, sugar, dry sherry, salt, Chinese five-spice powder and crushed fresh ginger.

Serves 4 • Preparation 10 minutes • Cooking 5 minutes

Pasta and Rice

Rice, the mainstay of half the world's population, is so easy to cook – just steam or boil and it's ready. Rice goes with everything, so it's incredibly simple to vary the flavor with nothing more than the addition of this or that ingredient. Pasta is almost equally versatile, and all the recipes in this chapter have been developed with the express purpose of making a tasty meal with a minimum of fuss, time and ingredients. Many pastas are also interchangeable – if the recipe calls for spaghetti but you use the fettuccine you already had in the cupboard, the recipe will still taste just as great.

Linguine with Pesto Cream

500g/1 lb linguine
1¼ cups heavy cream
½ cup basil pesto
80g/3 oz Parmesan cheese, shaved
1 teaspoon finely chopped parsley

1 Bring a large saucepan of salted water to a boil, add the pasta and cook for 8 minutes or until just firm in the center (al dente).
2 Place the cream, parsley and pesto in a large non-stick frying pan over medium heat. Gently simmer, stirring occasionally, for 3–4 minutes until thickened slightly.
3 Drain the pasta and return to the pan in which it was cooked. Pour over the pesto cream and toss to combine.
4 Top with Parmesan.

Serves 4 • Preparation 5 minutes • Cooking 15 minutes

Fusilli with Chicken and Tomato Cream Sauce

500g/1 lb fusilli
300g/10 oz chicken breast, thinly sliced
1 tablespoon vegetable oil
1¼ cups heavy cream
½ cup sun-dried tomato pesto

1 Bring a large saucepan of salted water to a boil, add the pasta and cook for 8 minutes or until just firm in the center (al dente). Drain, set aside and keep warm.
2 Heat the oil in a large non-stick frying pan on medium-high heat. Cook the chicken until browned, then remove from the pan and set aside. Reduce the heat to medium-low and add the cream and pesto. Gently simmer, stirring occasionally, for 3–4 minutes or until sauce has thickened slightly. Return the chicken to the pan and heat through.
3 Pour the sauce over the pasta and toss to combine.

Serves 4 • Preparation 5 minutes • Cooking 20 minutes

Capellini with Fresh Tomato Sauce

500g/1 lb capellini
12 tomatoes, chopped
1 teaspoon lemon juice
½ cup extra virgin olive oil
¾ cup fresh basil leaves, torn

1 Bring a large saucepan of salted water to a boil, add the pasta and cook for 8 minutes or until just firm in the center (al dente).
2 Place the tomatoes, lemon juice, oil and basil in a medium bowl. Stir to combine.
3 Drain the pasta and return to the pan in which it was cooked. Stir through the sauce.

Serves 4 • Preparation 5 minutes • Cooking 15 minutes

Spaghetti with Anchovies and Lemon

500g/1 lb spaghetti
50g/1–2 oz anchovies in oil, coarsely chopped
zest and juice of 2 lemons
1 clove garlic, crushed
1 cup Italian parsley, chopped

1 Bring a large saucepan of salted water to a boil, add the pasta and cook for 8 minutes or until just firm in the center (al dente). Drain, set aside and keep warm.
2 Place a large non-stick frying pan on medium-high heat. Add the anchovies and oil, lemon juice and zest, garlic and parsley, warm through. Add the pasta and toss to combine.

Serves 4 • Preparation 10 minutes • Cooking 15 minutes

Gnocchi with Tomato and Tarragon Sauce

800g/28 oz canned diced savoury tomatoes
8 sprigs tarragon, leaves removed and stalks discarded
½ teaspoon garlic salt
500g/1 lb potato gnocchi
80g/3 oz pecorino cheese, shaved

1 Place the tomatoes, tarragon and garlic salt in a medium heavy-based saucepan over medium heat. Gently simmer for 30 minutes until thickened and flavors have developed.
2 Bring a large saucepan of salted water to a boil, add the gnocchi and cook until it begins to float. Drain.
3 Toss the gnocchi with the sauce and stir in the cheese.

Serves 4 • Preparation 5 minutes • Cooking 15 minutes

Tortellini with Sage Butter

500g/1 lb meat-filled tortellini
6 tablespoons/100g butter
¾ cup fresh sage leaves
½ teaspoon freshly ground black pepper
80g/3 oz Parmesan cheese, grated

1 Bring a large saucepan of salted water to a boil, add the pasta and cook for 8 minutes or until just firm in the center (al dente).
2 Melt the butter in a large frying pan over medium-high heat. Add the sage and black pepper and cook for 30 seconds or until fragrant.
3 Toss to coat. Stir in Parmesan and serve.

Serves 4 • Preparation 5 minutes • Cooking 15 minutes

Pumpkin Risotto

1¼ kg/2½–3 lb pumpkin, peeled, seeded, and cut into 1 in/3cm pieces
400g/14 oz Arborio rice
4½ cups chicken stock, heated
120g/4 oz Parmesan cheese, freshly grated
1 teaspoon cream cheese

1 Preheat the oven to 400°F/200°C.
2 Place the pumpkin on an oven tray and bake for 20–30 minutes or until soft and golden.
3 Meanwhile, preheat a medium saucepan over medium-low heat. Add the rice and cook, stirring, for 1 minute. Reduce the heat to low, add ½ cup hot stock and cook, stirring constantly, until liquid is absorbed. Continue cooking in this way until all the stock is used and the rice is creamy and tender.
4 Add the pumpkin, cream cheese and half the Parmesan to the risotto and stir through to warm and combine.
5 Divide risotto among serving bowls and top with the remaining Parmesan.

Serves 4 • Preparation 10 minutes • Cooking 40–50 minutes

Scallop Risotto

400g/14 oz Arborio rice
4½ cups fish stock, heated
20 scallops, roe removed
8 Roma or plum tomatoes, diced
1 tablespoon finely grated Parmesan

1 Preheat a medium saucepan over medium-low heat. Add the rice and cook, stirring, for 1 minute. Reduce the heat to low, add ½ cup hot stock and cook, stirring constantly, until liquid is absorbed. Continue cooking in this way until all the stock is used and the rice is creamy and tender.

2 Heat a large non-stick frying pan on medium-high heat. Cook the scallops for 1 minute on each side, then transfer to a medium bowl.

3 Add the tomatoes, Parmesan and scallops to the risotto and stir through to warm and combine.

4 Divide the risotto evenly among four serving bowls.

Serves 4 • Preparation 10 minutes • Cooking 25 minutes

Mushroom and Pea Pilaf

200g/7 oz mushrooms, sliced
2 cups basmati rice
3 cups chicken stock
1 cup frozen peas
finely ground black pepper

1 Preheat a medium saucepan over medium heat. Add the mushroom and cook for 1–2 minutes. Add the rice and stock and bring to a boil. Reduce the heat to low, cover and cook for 20 minutes or until all the liquid has been absorbed.

2 Remove from the heat, add pepper and the peas and set aside, covered, for an additional 5 minutes. Stir through to combine and separate the grains. Divide evenly among four serving bowls.

Serves 4 • Preparation 5 minutes • Cooking 30 minutes

Chicken and Basil Risotto

300g/10 oz boneless, skinless chicken thighs, sliced
400g/14 oz Arborio rice
4½ cups chicken stock
1 cup basil leaves, torn
1 tablespoon finely grated Parmesan

1 Preheat a medium saucepan over medium heat. Add the chicken and cook for
   2–3 minutes on each side until browned. Transfer to a small bowl and set aside.
   Reduce the heat to low, add ½ cup hot stock and cook, stirring constantly, until
   liquid is absorbed. Continue cooking in this way until all the stock is used and
   the rice is creamy and tender.
2 Add the chicken, grated Parmesan and basil to the pan and stir through to
   warm and combine.

Serves 4 • Preparation 5 minutes • Cooking 25 minutes

Mexican Rice

2 cups long-grain white rice
400g/14 oz canned kidney beans, drained and rinsed
8 Roma or plum tomatoes, diced
3 Thai red chilies, halved lengthwise, seeded and finely chopped
1 clove garlic, crushed

1 Place the rice and 4 cups cold water in a large saucepan over high heat and bring to a boil. Reduce the heat to medium-low, cover and simmer for 12 minutes.
2 Remove from the heat, add the kidney beans, tomatoes, chilies and garlic and set aside, covered, for an additional 5 minutes. Stir through to combine and separate the grains.

Serves 4 • Preparation 10 minutes • Cooking 20 minutes

Pineapple Coconut Rice

2 cups basmati rice
300g/10 oz fresh pineapple, skinned and diced
½ cup fresh cilantro leaves
½ cup fresh mint leaves, finely sliced
¼ cup coconut milk

1 Combine the rice with 3 cups water in a saucepan. Bring to a boil, reduce heat to low, cover and cook for 15 minutes. Remove pan from heat, allow to stand covered for 10 minutes.

2 Spread the rice out on a tray. Refrigerate for 20 minutes or until cooled.

3 Place the rice, pineapple, cilantro, coconut milk and mint in a large bowl, stir to combine and serve.

Serves 4 • Preparation 30 minutes • Cooking 15 minutes

Coconut Rice

2 cups basmati rice
4 cinnamon sticks
6 cardamon pods, split
4 cups/1 liter coconut milk
2 teaspoons cream

1 Rinse the rice under cold water in a sieve. Place in a medium bowl and soak in cold water for 20 minutes.
2 Preheat a medium heavy-based saucepan over medium-low heat. Add the cinnamon and cardamon and cook for 2 minutes or until fragrant.
3 Drain the rice. Add the rice, coconut milk and cream to the pan and bring to a boil. Reduce the heat and simmer for 30 minutes or until the rice is tender and the liquid absorbed.

Serves 4 • Preparation 25 minutes • Cooking 35 minutes

Pistachio and Saffron Rice

2½ cups salted water
2 cups basmati rice
pinch of saffron threads
1 cup pistachios, coarsely chopped
¼ cup currants

1 Place salted water in a medium saucepan and bring to a boil. Add the rice and saffron and bring back to a boil. Reduce the heat to low, cover and simmer for 10 minutes. Remove from the heat and set aside with the lid on for an additional 10 minutes.

2 Add the pistachios and currants and stir through to combine and separate the grains.

Serves 4 • Preparation 5 minutes • Cooking 25 minutes

Vegetarian

With the terrific range of vegetables available all year round it is easy to select a series of recipes to please any palate – the hard part is to make them interesting using only a small number of additional ingredients. But don't worry, as we have developed the recipes in this chapter using minimum of ingredients for maximum taste. They can be used as an addition to a meal or as a meal in their own right.

Eggplant Stacks

2 large eggplant, cut into 8 rounds
6 garlic cloves, peeled
800g/28 oz canned diced Roma or plum tomatoes
½ cup olive tapenade
300g/10 oz goat cheese, sliced into 8 pieces

1 Preheat a grill pan to medium-high.

2 Rub the eggplant with the cut garlic cloves.

3 Grill the eggplant rounds for 2 minutes on each side or until charred and softened slightly. Transfer to a plate and set aside.

4 Preheat the oven to 375°F/190°C.

5 Place the tomatoes in a small saucepan over medium-low heat. Gently simmer for 5 minutes or until thickened.

6 Arrange 4 of the eggplant rounds on a baking sheet. Using half the tapenade, spread on each eggplant round, top with a slice of goat cheese. Create another layer using the rest of the eggplant, tapenade, goat cheese. Bake for 10 minutes or until the cheese is melted and golden. Bake for 10 minutes or until the cheese is golden.

7 To serve, spoon the tomatoes onto four serving dishes and place the eggplant stacks on top.

Serves 4 • Preparation 10 minutes • Cooking 20 minutes

Eggplant Rollatini

2 medium eggplant
750g/1½–2 lb ricotta cheese
¾ cup fresh basil, finely chopped
700g/25 oz tomato sauce
½ teaspoon Italian seasoning

1 Preheat the oven to 400°F/200°C.
2 Cut the eggplant lengthwise into ½ in/1cm-thick slices. Arrange the eggplant in a single layer on 2 large baking sheets. Bake for 10 minutes or until golden.
3 Place 600g/1¼ lb of the ricotta, Italian seasoning and ½ cup of the basil in a medium bowl and stir to combine.
4 Place a spoonful of ricotta mixture on an eggplant slice and roll up to enclose the filling. Place the roll seam-side down in a 9 x 13 in/30 x 20cm baking dish. Repeat the process with the remaining ricotta mixture and eggplant.
5 Pour the tomato sauce over the eggplant rolls. Sprinkle the remaining ricotta and basil over the top. Bake for 15 minutes or until heated through and ricotta is golden.

Serves 4 • Preparation 15 minutes • Cooking 25 minutes

Spanish Tortilla

750g/1½–2 lb potatoes, thinly sliced
⅓ cup olive oil
1 large onion, sliced
1 clove garlic, crushed
6 large eggs, lightly beaten

1 Preheat broiler.
2 Place the potato slices in a large saucepan and cover with cold water. Bring to a boil and cook for 2 minutes. Drain.
3 Place the oil in a large, non-stick, ovenproof pan over medium-high heat. Add the onion, garlic and potato slices and cooking, stirring, for 4–5 minutes or until browned. Decrease the heat to low and pour in the egg mixture. Cook without stirring for 4–6 minutes or until edges are firm.
4 Broil for 4–6 minutes, or until the eggs are set and slightly golden.
5 Cut into wedges and serve with crusty bread.

Serves 4 • Preparation 10 minutes • Cooking 20 minutes

Stuffed Tomatoes

4 large tomatoes
½ cup long-grain rice
100g/3½ oz mozzarella cheese, diced
1 tablespoon grated Parmesan
⅓ cup fresh basil leaves, finely chopped

1 Preheat the oven to 350°F/180°C.
2 Place the rice and 1 cup cold water in a small saucepan over high heat and bring to a boil. Reduce the heat to medium-low, cover and simmer for 12 minutes. Remove from the heat and stir through to separate the grains.
3 Cut the tops off the tomatoes and set aside. Scoop out the flesh and coarsely chop. Place the tomato flesh, mozzarella, Parmesan and basil in a medium bowl. Add the rice and stir to combine.
4 Place the tomato shells on a baking sheet and fill with the rice mixture. Put their tops back on and bake for 25–30 minutes until tomatoes are tender but still hold their shape.
5 Serve warm or cold.

Serves 4 • Preparation 10 minutes • Cooking 45 minutes

Carrot Beet Salad

8 medium carrots, peeled
3 large beets
2 tablespoons olive oil
2 teaspoons cumin seeds
1 teaspoon honey

1 Place a medium saucepan of salted water on high heat and bring to a boil.
2 Cut the beet from their stems and cook for 40 minutes or until tender. Drain and set aside to cool.
3 Peel the beets and cut into 1 in/2cm dice.
4 Place a large saucepan of salted water on high heat and bring to a boil.
5 Cook the carrots, whole, for 5–10 minutes until tender. Drain and set aside to cool, then cut into 1 in/2cm dice.
6 Heat the oil in a large non-stick frying pan on medium-high heat. Add the cumin seeds and cook for 1 minute until fragrant. Add the beets, carrot and honey and cook for an additional 2 minutes, stirring to coat.
7 Serve warm or cold.

Serves 4 • Preparation 15 minutes • Cooking 55 minutes

Nachos

800g/28 oz canned pinto beans
300g/10 oz salsa
1 teaspoon minced onion
250g/9 oz tortilla chips
150g/5 oz Cheddar cheese, grated

1 Preheat the oven to 375°F/190°C.
2 Place the beans and half the salsa and onion in a small saucepan over medium heat. Gently simmer for 3–4 minutes or until thickened slightly.
3 Arrange half of the corn chips in the base of four individual ovenproof serving bowls. Spoon half of the bean mixture on top and cover with the remaining chips. Top with the remaining bean mixture and sprinkle with cheese.
4 Bake for 5–10 minutes, until the cheese has melted.
5 Serve with sour cream, green onions and sliced jalapenos.

Serves 4 • Preparation 5 minutes • Cooking 15 minutes

Mushroom Stroganoff

500g/1 lb fettuccine
1 large onion, sliced
800g/28 oz button mushrooms, sliced
1¼ cups crème fraîche or sour cream
¼ cup heavy cream

1 Bring a large saucepan of salted water to a boil, add the pasta and cook
   for 8 minutes or until just firm in the center (al dente). Drain, set aside and
   keep warm.
2 Place a large non-stick frying pan on medium heat. Cook the onion and
   mushrooms, stirring occasionally, for 5 minutes or until softened and
   golden. Add the crème fraîche, cream and stir to combine. Lower the
   heat to medium-low and gently simmer for 5 minutes or until sauce has
   thickened slightly.

Serves 4 • Preparation 10 minutes • Cooking 20 minutes

Broccoli Quiche

1 sheet ready-made pie crust, thawed
500g/1¼ lb broccoli, cut into florets
8 large eggs, lightly beaten
1 tablespoon cream
200g/7 oz Gruyère cheese, thinly sliced

1 Preheat the oven to 400°F/200°C.

2 Line a 9 in/23cm pie plate with pie crust. Cover with parchment paper and fill with dried beans or rice. Place pie on a baking sheet and bake for 5–10 minutes until lightly golden. Remove the paper and beans/rice and let cool.

3 Place a medium saucepan of water on high heat and bring to a boil. Cook the broccoli for 1–2 minutes or until just tender, then drain.

4 Arrange broccoli on the bottom of the crust. Top with cheese and mixture of eggs and cream.

5 Bake for 30–35 minutes until set. Let stand for 10 minutes before slicing.

Serves 6 • Preparation 15 minutes • Cooking 50–55 minutes

Desserts

Let's not forget everyone's favorite part of the meal! We have come to the rescue with a brilliant selection of easy-to-prepare crowd pleasers, each still using only 5 ingredients. Don't worry about the calories or long prep time, most of these can be on the table in 10 minutes.

Profiteroles

250g/9 oz dark chocolate
1¼ cups heavy cream
¼ teaspoon orange blossom water (optional)
1 teaspoon vanilla extract
12 premade cream puffs*

1 Melt the chocolate and ¼ cup of the cream together in a small heatproof bowl over a saucepan of barely simmering water. Stir to combine and set aside to cool.

2 Whip the remaining cream with the vanilla and orange blossom water in a small bowl using an electric mixer until soft peaks form. Spoon the cream into a pastry bag fitted with a round nozzle.

3 Cut a hole big enough to fit the piping nozzle in the base of the cream puffs.Pipe cream into cream puffs, drizzle chocolate sauce over each, and serve immediately.

*Cream puffs can be bought ready-made from the bakery section of your local supermarket.

Serves 4 • Preparation 15 minutes

Chocolate Mousse

3 large eggs, separated
3 teaspoons dark brown sugar
100g/3½ oz dark chocolate
1½ cups heavy cream
1 teaspoon olive oil

1 Whisk the egg yolks and sugar together in a small heatproof bowl. Place the bowl over a saucepan of barely simmering water and continue whisking until thick and creamy. Remove from the heat.

2 Put the chocolate in a small heatproof bowl and place over the simmering water to melt, whisk olive oil into the melted chocolate and pour into the egg yolk mixture, stir to combine and set aside to cool.

3 Whip 1 cup of the cream in a small bowl until soft peaks form. In a separate bowl, whisk the egg whites until soft peaks form. Fold the cream and whites together.

4 Stir 1 spoonful of the egg white mixture into the chocolate. Add the remaining whites and gently fold until combined. Pour the mousse into serving cups or bowls. Cover with plastic wrap and refrigerate for 2 hours or until required.

5 Whip the remaining cream in a small bowl. Spoon into a pastry bag fitted with a star nozzle. Pipe a small amount on top of each mousse. Decorate with shaved extra chocolate.

Serves 4 • Preparation 2 hours 25 minutes

Watermelon Granita

1 cup water
¾ cup sugar
juice of 2 limes
juice of 1 lemon
1kg/2 lb watermelon, peeled, seeded and cut into pieces

1 Place the water, sugar and lime and lemon juices in a small saucepan over medium heat and bring to a boil. Reduce the heat and simmer, stirring occasionally, until the sugar has dissolved. Add the watermelon and simmer for 3 minutes. Transfer to a bowl and refrigerate until cooled. Pour watermelon mixture into a food processor and blend until puréed.

2 Pour the liquid into a 9 x 13 in/20 x 30cm pan. Cover with plastic wrap.

3 Freeze for 2 hours. Remove from the freezer and use a fork to break up the granita into large crystals. Return to the freezer for 1 hour, then break up with a fork again. Repeat three more times until crystals are completely frozen.

4 Spoon the granita into serving glasses and serve immediately.

Serves 6 • Preparation 6 hours 10 minutes • Cooking 5 minutes

Chocolate Orange Sorbet

2¾ cups water
1 cup sugar
1 cup cocoa powder
zest of 2 oranges
½ teaspoon orange liqueur

1 Place the water and sugar in a medium saucepan over medium-high heat and bring to a boil. Reduce the heat and simmer, stirring occasionally, until the sugar has dissolved.
2 Add the cocoa powder and orange zest, orange liqueur and simmer gently for 15 minutes. Remove from the heat and strain through a fine mesh sieve. Discard the orange zest.
3 Refrigerate until cooled.
4 Pour the cooled liquid into an ice maker and churn until the sorbet starts to become firm. Serve immediately or transfer to a container and freeze until required.

Serves 4 • Preparation 1 hour

Zabaglione

4 large egg yolks
¼ cup sugar
¼ teaspoon vanilla extract
¼ cup Marsala or dessert wine
8 lady fingers

1 Place the egg yolks, sugar and vanilla in a medium heatproof bowl. Whisk the yolks until thick and creamy. Gradually add the Marsala, whisking to combine.
2 Place the bowl over a saucepan of barely simmering water. Cook, whisking continuously, for 10 minutes, until thick enough to coat the back of a spoon.
3 Pour into 4 serving glasses. Serve immediately with lady fingers on the side.

Serves 4 • Preparation 5 minutes • Cooking 10 minutes

Banana and Chocolate Pavlovas

1 cup crème fraîche
1 teaspoon Cointreau
4 small meringues
1 large banana, thinly sliced diagonally
50g/2 oz dark chocolate

1 Mix the Cointreau into the crème fraîche until combined.
2 Spoon the crème fraîche onto the meringues. Arrange slices of banana decoratively on top. Create chocolate curls using a vegetable peeler and stack on top.
3 Place onto serving plates and serve immediately.

Serves 4 • Preparation 10 minutes

Chocolate and Hazelnut Tart

1 sheet ready-made pie crust, thawed
250g/9 oz dark chocolate
1 cup heavy cream
1 cup hazelnuts, lightly toasted and coarsely chopped
½ teaspoon Frangellico (hazelnut liqueur)

1 Preheat the oven to 350°F/180°C.

2 Line a pie plate with the pie crust. Refrigerate for 10 minutes.

3 Cover pie crust with parchment paper and fill with dried beans or rice. Place pie on a baking sheet and bake for 5–10 minutes until lightly golden. Remove the paper and beans/rice and bake for an additional 10 minutes or until the center is cooked through.

4 Put the chocolate and cream into a small heatproof bowl. Place over a saucepan of barely simmering water and melt, stirring occasionally until smooth. Stir ¾ cup of the hazelnuts and the Frangellico into the chocolate mixture and pour into the baked pie crust. Refrigerate for 2 hours or until set.

5 Decorate the tart with the remaining hazelnuts.

Serves 6–8 • Preparation 2 hours 15 minutes • Cooking 20 minutes

Crème Brûlée

2½ cups heavy cream
1 vanilla bean, split lengthwise
6 large egg yolks
½ cup sugar
1 teaspoon finely grated orange zest

1 Preheat the oven to 250°F/120°C.
2 Place the cream, vanilla pod and seeds in a small saucepan over medium heat and bring to scalding point. Remove from the heat and set aside to infuse for 10 minutes.
3 Place the egg yolks and half the sugar in a medium bowl. Whisk until pale and creamy.
4 Remove the vanilla bean from the cream and discard. Gradually pour the hot cream into the egg mixture, stirring with a wooden spoon to combine. Strain the custard mixture through a fine mesh sieve and mix through orange zest
5 Pour the custard into four one cup ovenproof ramekins. Place the ramekins in a deep roasting pan. Pour boiling water into the pan to come halfway up the side of the ramekins, then cover the pan loosely with foil. Place in the oven and bake for 40 minutes or until custards are set but still slightly wobbly.
6 Carefully remove the ramekins from the pan and set aside to cool. Cover with plastic wrap and refrigerate for 4 hours or until required.
7 Preheat the broiler.
8 Sprinkle the remaining sugar evenly over the top of each custard. Broil until sugar is caramelized and brown. You can also use a small kitchen blowtorch.

Serves 4 • Preparation 4 hours 30 minutes • Cooking 40 minutes

Raspberry Panna Cotta

½ cup sugar
2 cups heavy cream
15g/½ oz gelatin sheets
450g/1 oz fresh raspberries
1 teaspoon raspberry liqueur

1   Place the sugar and half the cream in a small saucepan and gently heat to just below simmering point – do not boil. Remove from the heat.

2   Put the gelatin sheets into a bowl, cover with cold water and leave for 5 minutes or until softened. Drain and squeeze out the excess liquid. Add the gelatin to the cooked cream and stir until it has dissolved. Set aside to cool.

3   Place the raspberries in a food processor and blend until puréed. Strain through a fine mesh sieve and discard the seeds, stir in raspberry liqueur. Add the purée to the cooked cream and stir to combine.

4   Whip the remaining cream in a small bowl until soft peaks form. Add the whipped cream to the raspberry cream mixture and fold through.

5   Pour the raspberry cream mixture into four 1-cup plastic or metal moulds. Place moulds onto a tray and refrigerate for 4 hours or until required.

6   To serve, run a small knife around the edge of the panna cotta to loosen and invert onto serving plates.

Serves 4 • Preparation 4 hours 20 minutes • Cooking 5 minutes

Lemon Napoleon

2 sheets frozen puff pastry, thawed
½ cup heavy cream
½ cup lemon curd
1 tablespoon powdered sugar
½ teaspoon lemon juice

1 Preheat the oven to 400°F/200°C.
2 Cut each sheet of puff pastry into six rectangles (2½ x 5 in/6 x 12cm). Lay the pastry on two baking sheets and bake for 10–15 minutes until puffed and golden brown. Remove from the oven, flatten slightly and leave to cool.
3 Whip the cream in a small bowl until soft peaks form. Add the lemon juice to the lemon curd and stir to combine. Mix lemon curd mixture into cream.
4 Spread half of the lemon cream over four pieces of the pastry. Top with another piece of pastry and repeat the process, finishing with the last pastry sheet.
5 Dust with powdered sugar and serve immediately.

Serves 4 • Preparation 15 minutes • Cooking 15 minutes

Custard Tart

1 sheet ready-made pie crust, thawed
1 cups milk
½ cup heavy cream
2 large eggs, plus 1 large egg yolk
2 tablespoons sugar

1 Preheat the oven to 350°F/180°C.

2 Line a pie plate with pie crust and refrigerate for 10 minutes.

3 Cover the pie crust with parchment paper and fill with dried beans or rice. Place pie on a baking sheet and bake for 5–10 minutes until lightly golden. Remove the paper and beans/rice and let cool.

4 Reduce the oven temperature to 325°F/160°C.

5 Place the milk, cream, eggs, egg yolk and sugar in a medium bowl and whisk to combine. Pour the mixture into the crust and return to the oven to cook for 20 minutes or until custard is set. Remove from the oven and leave to cool for 10 minutes. Refrigerate for 2 hours or until required.

Serves 6 • Preparation 2 hours 10 minutes • Cooking 40 minutes

Lemon Lime Sorbet

2 cups water
80g/3 oz sugar
juice of 5 limes
juice of 1 lemon
¼ cup gin

1 Place the water, sugar lemon and lime juice in a small saucepan over medium heat and bring to a boil. Reduce the heat and simmer, stirring occasionally, until the sugar has dissolved. Transfer to a bowl and refrigerate until cooled.

2 Pour the cooled liquid into an ice-maker and churn until the sorbet starts to become firm. Add the gin and churn for an additional 5 minutes until firm again. Serve immediately or transfer to a container and freeze until required.

Serves 4 • Preparation 30 minutes • Cooking 5 minutes

Index